HENRY RANKIN POORE

COMPOSITION
IN ART

STERLING
PUBLISHING CO., INC. NEW YORK

Oak Tree Press Co., Ltd.
London & Sydney

ART BOOKS

Abstract Art

Abstract Landscape Painting

Bridgman's Complete Guide to Drawing from Life

Carlson's Guide to Landscape Painting

Color in Oil Painting

Composition in Art

Etching (and Other Intaglio Techniques)

Experiments in Modern Art

Painting the Sea

Sculpture for Beginners

Watercolor Painting for Beginner

Adapted by Anne Egan

Schematics by Shizu Matsuda

1971 Printing

Copyright © 1967 by Sterling Publishing Co., Inc.
419 Park Avenue South, New York, N.Y. 10016
British edition published by Oak Tree Press Co., Ltd., Nassau, Bahamas
Distributed in Australia by Oak Tree Press Co., Ltd.,
P.O. Box 34, Brickfield Hill, Sydney 2000, N.S.W.
Distributed in the United Kingdom and elsewhere in the British Commonwealth
by Ward Lock Ltd., 116 Baker Street, London W 1
Originally published under the title
"Pictorial Composition and the Critical Judgment of Pictures"
Manufactured in the United States of America
All rights reserved
Library of Congress Catalog Card No.: 66-25199
ISBN 0-8069-5084-6   UK 7061 2084 1
5085-4

Contents

"Giovanni Arnolfini and His Wife" by Jan van Eyck. National Gallery, London.

1. The Importance of Balance

AN ARTIST AT WORK usually stands at his easel and views his picture at various distances, looks at it over his shoulder, looks at it in reverse through a mirror, turns it upside-down at times, develops it with dots or spots of color here and there. He puts in points of accent carefully and often changes them.

Why does he do all this? He is striving for BALANCE or equipoise. The sensitive eye of artist and viewer tests every picture for balance, a judgment usually rendered naturally by everyone, with or without knowledge of artistic laws.

After the picture has been finished, why does an artist often feel compelled to create an accent on one side or weaken an obtrusive point on the other side of his canvas?

Take a painting which has lived long enough to be considered good by everyone. Subject it to the following test: Find the actual middle of the picture and pass a vertical and horizontal line through it. The vertical division is the more important, as the natural balance is on the sides of a central support. The central point of the canvas is also the actual pivot of the picture, and round such a point the various components group themselves, pulling and

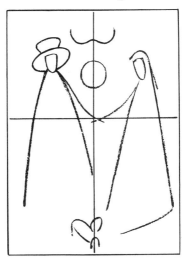

1. A diagram of the painting on the opposite page clearly shows complete balance round the exact middle. The joined hands act as a pivot point for the whole composition.

5

"Madonna di San Sisto" by Raphael. Gallery, Dresden.

2. Classical balance requires equal measures on each side of a central figure or object—and also ideally displays balancing elements from top to bottom. The visual effect is that of the scales above. For each part, there must be a corresponding part to keep the scales from teetering.

battling for their share of attention. The *satisfactory* picture shows as much design of balance on one side as the other, and the completely balanced picture displays this equipoise above and below the horizontal line as well.

Every item of a picture has a degree of PULLING POWER, as though each object were a magnet of some potency or strength. Each has attraction for the eye. While each draws attention to itself, it detracts from every other part proportionately. On the principle of the STEELYARD (which we will discuss in detail later), the farther from the middle and more isolated an object is, the greater its weight or attraction. In the balance of a picture, you will find that a very important object placed but a short distance from the middle will be balanced by a very small object on the other side of this central point and *further removed from it.* The whole pictorial interest may be on one side of a picture. The

6

other side may be practically useless, may have no picturesqueness or story to tell. Its reason for existing will be for balance alone.

The very small object we spoke of may be an accent or line of attraction, or may be no more than a spiritual quality. A strong feeling of gloom, or light or dark, can be enough for the eye to dwell on. But if all of the subject is on one side of the middle and the other side depends for its existence on only a balancing space or accent, why not cut it off? Try! You will have the entire subject in one-half the former space, but its harmony or balance will depend on its equipoise when pivoted on a new central point.

Balance of the steelyard

Make this test on any painting: Cut away everything on one side in an attempt to place the main subject in the exact middle. See if the picture composes well in this shape. Then re-add to the

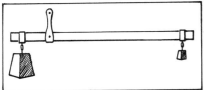

"Robert Andrew and Wife" by Thomas Gainsborough. National Gallery, London.

3. *The principle of the steelyard, a small weight balancing a large weight, is seen in this composition. The tree acts as a fulcrum for the large mass at the left (which is also the subject) and the lighter weight of the hay and trees at the right, whose importance is for balance alone.*

7

 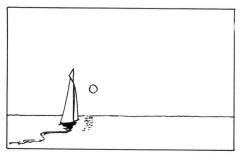

4. When you have completed a picture, try cutting off various parts of it to determine whether you have achieved a balanced composition. Here, the last drawing exhibits the balance necessary when a subject is on one side. The tiny steamer in the distance pulls the entire picture together. Note how the wake of the sailing yacht leads the eye into the picture and adds depth.

side and see how the central point has shifted. Note whether the subject is close to the pivot point and whether it demands more balance now that the side is added back. If the main subject has weight enough, leave it alone—the over-scientific enthusiast might err here. The artist will often add a vertical figure to oppose a horizontal, or will catch and turn the line of a shadow on a wall into the line of the floor. The governing principle here is: Where the subject of a picture is on one side of the middle, it must be close to the pivot point. If it departs from the middle, it must show positive anchorage to the other side.

Not every good picture can show *complete* balance, but when the artist striving for balance achieves it, the picture is that much better. By applying the simple test of elimination of overweighted parts (adding items where needed), you will find whether or not the composition will improve. The small balancing weight of the steelyard should not become a point that causes divided interest.

It is easy to recognize a good composition. To tell why it is good may be difficult. To tell how it could be made better is what the artist wants to know. When in doubt, weigh out your picture in balances, keeping in mind the principle of the steelyard to cover the items in the depth as well as across the breadth of your picture, as in Brueghel's "Hunters in the Snow."

5. The main group is just to the left of the middle, and is balanced by the small figure and the height and mass of the building. Place your hand over the right side of the picture—the effect is like a seesaw or teeter-totter when one person leaves it suddenly, causing the other to go crashing down.

"A Dutch Courtyard" by Pieter de Hooch. National Gallery of Art, Washington, D.C. Mellon Collection.

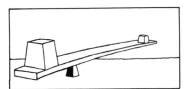

6. The steelyard in depth as well as breadth. Balance in more than one dimension is vital to good composition.

"Hunters in the Snow" by Pieter Brueghel, the Elder. Kunsthistorisches Museum, Vienna.

Rules

- Every picture is a collection of units or items.
- Every unit has a given value.
- The value of a unit depends on its attraction, and its attraction varies according to placement.
- A unit near the edge has more attraction than the same unit at the middle.
- Every part of the picture space has some attraction.
- Space without detail may possess attraction by gradation and by suggestion.
- A unit of attraction in an otherwise empty space has more weight through isolation than when placed with other units.
- A black unit on white or a white unit on black has more attraction than the same unit on grey.
- The value of a black or a white unit is proportionate also to the size of the space that contrasts with it.
- A unit in the foreground has less weight than the same one in the distance.
- Two or more associated units may be reckoned as one. Their UNITED CENTRAL POINT is the point on which they balance with others.

Scale of attraction

There is balance of Line (Illustration 7), of Mass (Illustration 8), of Light and Dark (Illustration 9), and of Measure (Illustration 10). A scale of attraction measures how much each possesses. Many pictures exhibit these balances in combination.

In every composition the eye should cross the central division at least once. This creates equipoise or balance of parts. In the survey of a picture, the eye naturally shifts from the focus of interest, which may be on one side, to the other side of the canvas. If something is there to receive it, the balance which the eye seeks is gratified. If it finds nothing, the artist must create something.

In a landscape, the eye may be attracted from trees to houses and rest there, or it may move to the other half of the picture *if* something has been created to draw it there. What is known as DIVIDED INTEREST in a picture is nothing more than the doubt created by a false arrangement, in which too great an attraction is used where less weight is required. The artist must be the judge,

7. This circular composition represents an excellent balance of lines. The focal point of the picture is where the hands join, and it is towards this point in each quadrant that linear movement is directed. The diagram could be carried even further to represent the spokes of a wheel.

"Marriage of Bacchus and Ariadne" by Tintoretto.

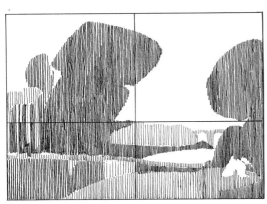

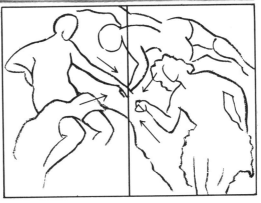

8. Balance of mass as shown here is achieved by distribution of light and dark areas. The greater weight on the left is offset by the area of interest on the right, principally by the small white mass of the group— another application of the steelyard.

"Landscape with the Rest on the Flight to Egypt" by Claude Lorraine. Hermitage, Leningrad.

11

Sketch based on Caravaggio's "Youth Bitten by a Lizard."

9. Balance of light and dark is beautifully expressed in all of Caravaggio's work. Here, nearly blinding light and dark shadow play against each other, even in the face which is perfectly divided into two distinct areas. Note also the glass vase which could be a mirror reflection of the face.

but no one can ignore the threat of divided interest when trying to obtain unity.

The question of *degree* is important. In an attempt to create a balance on the opposite side of a vertical, the tendency is to use too heavy a weight. A subject can sometimes take its place well to one side, making another item seem redundant. A two-part test can be used: If the questionable half is either cut off or greatly elongated, will the picture still survive without damage?

Sketch based on Jean Léon Gérôme's "Lion in the Desert."

10. Three isolated spots and one line of attraction combine to form balance of equal measures. The eye falls on the lion, then follows the path to the right to the patch of tall grass and on back to the dark mass of hills.

In filling a vase with flowers you strive for both unity and balance in the arrangement. If, however, color combination, massing or accent is lacking, the result is disturbing and disharmonious. To be effective in a frame, a picture needs balance and unity, just as much as a flower arrangement. The eye finds repose and delight in a perfect balance of elements, brought into combination and bound together by the girdle of the frame.

A picture should be able to hang from its exact middle. A perfect composition will not cause the viewer to turn his head to a false angle in the picture. Pictures that stand the test of time demand this.

Just as the BALANCE OF THE FIGURE dominates all other considerations in sculpting or painting the human form, so does the equipoise (balance of parts) of the picture become the chief consideration in composition. In the same way that the sculpture balances its weight over its point of support, so the picture balances upon a fulcrum or pivot point from which large and small masses spread with the same delicate adjustment.

11. An ideal balance of parts where the entire picture hangs from the exact middle. The top of the umbrella acts as a pivot from which the various parts subtly radiate.

"Hideyoshi Amusing Himself with his Five Concubines" by Kitagawa Utamaro.

13

"Summer" by Claude Monet. Staatsgalerie, Stuttgart.

12. The wide line of the meadows, the narrower line of the hills and the broad expanse of sky are perfectly balanced by three vertical elements—the tall trees in the foreground, the little tree and the distant row of trees.

Vertical and horizontal balance

LATERAL (HORIZONTAL) BALANCE is all-important to the upright subject. The significance of horizontal balance is best understood, however, in the example of a landscape, because it has extended perspective. Here the balance is like a see-saw. When you have a long space from foreground to distance, filled with varying degrees of interest, it is apparent how easily one end may become too heavy for the other. The artist must temper such a chain of items until equipoise is attained.

The importance of balance varies according to the number of units to be composed. Much greater liberty may be taken in settling a single figure into its picture-space than when the composition involves many figures. The mind hardly considers balance until it notes a complication of many units.

14

Two main lines will start a composition, *if they touch or cross.*
After that you must work in the balances as the picture hangs.
However, not until you have brought the picture to the *last* stage
of finished detail, can you complete the balance. What you conceived of originally in general outline may end up all askew. The
scheme of light and dark in one or two flat tones without a BALANCE
OF GRADATION will as many times prove false as true before the
picture is complete. Some artists paint important pictures from
notebook sketches, put down "hot," that is, when the impression
is fresh. These often convey more of the essence of the subject
than the faithful "study" done at leisure.

*13. The simplest of verticals and horizontals form this composition—one main broad band
and two verticals bisecting it. The placement of the tree at the left is crucial to the
perspective.*

"Chateau of Amboise" by Raoul Dufy. Collection, The Museum of Modern Art, New York. Loula D. Lasker Bequest.

"The Washington Family" by Edward Savage. National Gallery of Art, Washington, D.C.   Mellon Collection.

14. The natural axis penetrates the exact middle of this painting, in depth as well as vertically and horizontally.

15. The lack of depth here creates an axial plane on the surface of the painting. The figures seem to move in two dimensions only, creating a unified balance across the middle from top to bottom and from side to side, which is accented by the basic circular plan.

"Dance" (first version) by Henri Matisse. Collection, Museum of Modern Art, New York.
Gift of Nelson A. Rockefeller in honor of Alfred H. Barr, Jr.

16. The axial planes form where the horizon and the vertical cliffs meet. A line along the shore at the right and another along the low rocks at the left would both lead into the axial pivot. It is these lines that draw us into the picture.

The natural axis

In varying degrees, pictures express what may be termed a NATURAL AXIS, an axis on which the picture components are arranged in a balanced composition. This axis is the visible or imaginary line which the eye accepts. If, for instance, there is only one figure or group with an opening or point of attraction through the background diverting the eye to it, then this line of direction becomes the axis. The axis not only connects two points within the picture, but pierces it. The near end of the shaft has much to do with this balance.

Balance *across the middle* creates unity in the picture, limiting it within its frame. We can see it easily where the subject has little depth of background. We recognize balance of movement *on the axis* when the axis reaches far in. We can feel the subject revolving on its pivot, perhaps stretching one arm towards us while the other arm penetrates the visible or invisible distance.

17

"The Boating Party" by Mary Cassatt. National Gallery of Art, Washington, D.C.   Chester Dale Collection.

17. The axis of this composition is well marked. The baby is the focal point or pivot round which the figures and objects almost visibly revolve. Note how the oar and the man's arm effectively are carried over—the line of the oar to his hat; the line of the arm through the sail.

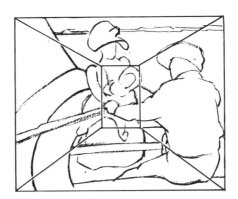

Balance constructed over this axis will bring the artist to as unified a result as will the use of the steelyard on the central vertical line. In the axis method there is less restraint, so when the axis is well marked, it is best to take it. Not every subject develops it. But when the axis *is* found, its force should be modified by opposed lines or measures on one or both sides.

18

"School of Athens" by Raphael. Camera della Segnatura, Vatican, Rome.

18. An ideal formal arrangement. The composition could be extended indefinitely on either side. Study carefully the balancing elements which vary only slightly except in degree. Measure for measure is the keynote.

Apparent or formal balance

Raphael is a convenient master with whom to begin a study of composition. His style was influenced by certain considerations—he heeded the warning provided by the pitfalls of composition into which his predecessors had fallen, and he had confidence that absolutely formal balance was utterly safe. He was influenced too by the environment for which most of his works were produced. His was an architectural plan of arrangement, and this well suited the dignity of his subjects.

Raphael was, therefore, the chief exponent of FORMAL COM-POSITION. His plan involved placing the figure of greatest importance in the middle—with balancing figures on either side. He deliberately weakened his set formality with objects which slightly changed the balance in kind or degree. The whole arrangement resembled that of an army in battle array, with its middle, flanks and skirmish-

19

19. This early miniature displays equal weighted sides. A vertical line through the middle would create a near mirror image. An interesting concession to the structural lack of depth has been made in the left corner of the throne roof and in the angular placement of the throne itself.

ers. The BALANCE OF EQUAL MEASURES, seen in his "Sistine Madonna" (Illustration 2), is conspicuous in early ecclesiastical works, notably "The Last Supper" of Leonardo, in which two groups of three persons each are posed on either side of the pivotal figure.

This has become the standard arrangement for all classical balanced pictorial composition. The doubling of objects on either side of a central figure not only gives the main subject importance, but contributes the peace, symmetry and solemnity appropriate to religious feeling and decorum. One objection to this plan of balance is that it divides the picture into equal parts, neither one having precedence, and often the subdivisions are continued indefinitely. For this reason this arrangement has no place in genre art.

A more objectionable form of central balance is that in which the middle is of little importance—this results in cutting the picture into two parts for no reason. Donatello's "Herod's Feast" is a good example. In this composition the formality of the

"The Last Supper" by Leonardo da Vinci. Santa Maria delle Grazie, Milan. Photograph courtesy of Italian State Tourist Office.

20. An excellent example of the balance of equal measures is seen here where Christ is exactly placed in the middle with two groups of three apostles on either side. Note, too, the placement of the small items on the table. The graceful mobile postures of the apostles prevent what could have been a stiff, uninspired composition.

21. Compare with Leonardo's "Last Supper." The basic structure is formal, with corresponding elements on either side of a central point, which here has no importance whatever. The eye tends to pass right through the middle. The isolated group on the right is joined to the figure of Herod at the left only by the direction of their glances. They could easily be cut off. The subject itself, John the Baptist's head presented to Herod, is a moment of horror and does not lend itself to a plan of formal balance, which conveys dignity and decorum.

"Herod's Feast" by Donatello. Gilt bronze relief from a font in S. Giovanni, Siena.

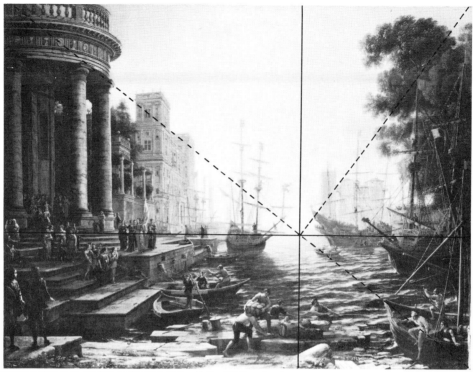

"Embarkation of St. Ursula" by Claude Lorraine. National Gallery, London.

22. The application of the classic form of construction, the "golden mean," is best seen in many of the works of Lorraine who consciously made use of it. It is interesting to apply this test to recent compositions, which were most likely not conceived with the golden mean in mind, but which, on analysis, bear out the principle. See John Marin's "Lower Manhattan," Illustration 24.

structure is not appropriate to the theme. In all forms except classic, the artist should try to conceal the balance over the middle.

Points equidistant from any two sides are also weak points. Inequalities in distance should bear a mathematical ratio to each other, as one-third and two-thirds, or two-fifths and three-fifths.

A canvas can also be divided according to the "golden mean." The principle of the golden mean was developed by the ancient Greeks who applied it to the designing of their temples.

On a rectangular canvas, connect two opposing corners with a diagonal. From this diagonal construct a vertical to one of the remaining corners. Through the point where the vertical meets the diagonal, draw two lines, each connecting two sides of the rectangle. The divisions that result are excellent bases for construction. In addition, they each, in turn, can be divided by the same means, and a painting so conceived will inevitably contain the most pleasing and balanced proportions possible.

This proportional division of the picture can be seen in the best of Claude Lorraine's landscapes, as it was one of his principal methods of construction. (See Illustration 22.)

Balance by opposition of line

A series of oppositional lines has variety and is therefore picturesque. In this sense, picturesqueness is variety in unity. The lines of a long road in perspective offer an easy path for the eye. However, the eye is far more interested in threading its way over a track lost then found, lost and found again. In time, you arrive from *a* to *z* by one route as surely as by the other, but in one the journey has been more intriguing.

Imagine a hillside and sky as a picture. The hillside is without detail, the sky a blank. The first item introduced attracts the eye.

"The Houses of Parliament, Sunset" by Claude Monet. National Gallery of Art, Washington, D.C. Chester Dale Collection.

23. The two principal lines formed by the base of the mass of buildings and the large vertical structure are repeated and counteracted by the small vertical of the figure and the horizontal of the boat.

23

The second and third are joined with the first. If they parallel the line of the hillside they do nothing towards the development of the picture. Rather, they harm it by creating a feeling of monotony. On the other hand, if they are placed in sky and land in such a manner as to *oppose* this line, they help send the eye on its travels.

Compare for instance the artist with the fencer. The fencer makes long, sweeping strokes that simply must be parried, or opposed, quite decisively; the *riposte* must also be parried. Such a bout is a striking composition of two men and two minds in which the unity of the whole and the unity of the parts are both maintained by the BALANCE OF OPPOSED MEASURES. To the fencer, a feeling of opposition is second nature. The painter in turn stands off, brush in hand, and fights his subject to the finish, the force of one stroke neutralizing and parrying another. This is true, not only of color composition where the scheme is to produce harmony by opposition of colors, but also of linear composition.

"Lower Manhattan," 1920, by John Marin. Collection, The Museum of Modern Art, New York. Philip L. Goodwin Collection.

24. The linear elements of this watercolor—verticals and diagonals—successfully oppose each other to form a finely balanced composition without benefit of strong horizontals.

"Spanish Dancing Girl" by Henri de Toulouse-Lautrec Monfa. Private collection.

25. Just as a leading line carries us through a painting, so can spots. The immediate attraction of the dark spot on the floor draws us to an opposing, but equivalent, spot—the girl's hair. The imaginary line between these two accents is carried through the arm, but we are immediately drawn back by the strength of the two dark patches.

Balance by opposition of spots

While the eye will follow a line more readily, spots or accents, for the most part, can be used in much the same way. The spot is a potent force of attraction. Its subtlety is often worth more than the simple strength of the line.

The advantage of the spot is that it creates BALANCE BY TRAN-SITION. Since this is one of the most important principles in landscape composition, imagine the following scene: A simple hillside with a background of a dense mass of trees, presenting a flat and an upright plane. However, until the eye is carried into and beyond the line of juncture of these two planes, their opposition to each other accomplishes very little, other than affording a strong contrast of light and shade. The eye must be coaxed into travelling gradually through the composition, from a pathway or other object

25

"Camden Mountain Across the Bay" by John Marin. Collection, The Museum of Modern Art, New York. Gift of Abby Aldrich Rockefeller.

26. Note the force and simplicity of the accents throughout. Balance and transition are one in this attractive scene. Study the oppositional and cohesive elements, such as the sun and the dark corresponding spot at the base of the mountain.

in front of, or on the hill, through the trees and up to the sky. This illustration is extremely simple in nature, but it is of the utmost importance because it concerns both lateral and perspective balance.

Transition of line

Often more effective than opposition (as the crossbar is more effective for strength than the bar supported on only one side) is TRANSITION. In this type of balance, the same object is carried across or delivered to another object which crosses a line or space. In fact, transitional line is so powerful that it should be used with great care.

In landscape, the transitional line from land into sky is often

27. *We are effectively drawn into this scene with its many layers of horizontals by the road which crosses the canvas on an angle. Eliminate the road, and your eye will find the transition from land to sky or sky to land difficult. The road finds its equal in the bars of light in the sky.*

"Landscape" by Albert Pinkham Ryder, The Metropolitan Museum of Art, New York. Gift of Frederick Kuhne.

"The Tugboat" by Alfred Sisley.   Petit Palais, Paris. Photo by J. E. Bulloz.

28. *A more subtle transition: here from the line of the shore through the trees and up. The added touch of the tugboat stacks and column of smoke strengthens the transitional upward forces. The mass on the left is well balanced by the various linear elements on the right.*

"Old Man and his Grandson" by Ghirlandaio. Service photographique, Chateau de Versailles, France.

29. (Left) Line can draw you out of the picture with scarcely a glance at the subject. The long curving perspective of the detailed landscape is distracting and unnecessary. This is not transition, but escape.

30. (Right) Compare with above. Although the eye travels across the line of figures and then to the opening background where it could easily get lost, the line is saved by the figure in the door whose gaze turns us back to the subject.

"Las Meninas" by Diego Velazquez. Museo del Prado, Madrid.

unrealistic and undesirable. The very nature and feeling of the subject itself may automatically reject such a union. Here, the principle only should be hinted at. In the case of a sunset sky and a beach, where the clouds float as parallel bars above the horizon, conveying the quality of a quiet and windless closing of day, a transitional line such as a tree, mast or spire may not be available. Oppositional spots or lines attracting the vision into the land and thus diverting it from the horizontals are the only recourse.

In Ghirlandaio's "Old Man and His Grandson," the long perspective line beyond the figures, continuing the lines of the foreground, directs the vision right through the subject, carrying

28

"Syndics of the Cloth Hall" by Rembrandt van Rijn. Rijks Museum, Amsterdam.

31. A successful linear grouping. The eye might easily be led across and out; however, the line of transition pauses first at the standing figure and then at the less-defined man in the rear. Thus, we are led across and back in an elliptical line of movement.

it out of the picture. If you are trying to focus your attention on the subject, you feel the interruption and annoyance of this unnecessary landscape. The Italian school of the Renaissance often weakened the force of its portraits and figure pictures by elaborate settings which they seemed helpless to cope with. In Velasquez, we frequently find simplicity of background which saves the entire interest for the subject; but even he makes the same error in some of his compositions.

In one of the greatest of Rembrandt's portrait groups, "The Syndics," he was faced with the problem of placing six figures. Four are seated at the far side of a table looking towards us; the fifth, on the near side, rises and looks at us. His head, higher than those of the row of four, breaks this line of formality; but the depth and perspective of the picture is not achieved until a figure standing in the background is added. This produces—from the foreground figure, through one of the seated figures—the transitional line which pulls the composition forwards and backwards and makes a circular composition of what was originally a line sweeping across the entire canvas.

"Steamer in Snowstorm" by Joseph Mallord William Turner. Tate Gallery, London.

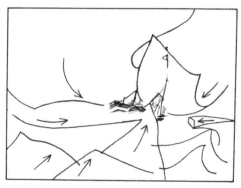

32. A masterful example of balance achieved through gradation. The powerful suggestion of movement through the use of lights and darks draws the eye through the painting. The linear impulses at the same time lead us to the subject—the storm-tossed boat.

Balance by gradation

Gradation will be mentioned later in another connection, but as a force in balance it must be noted here. It does not matter *how* the tone grades, from light to dark or the reverse, because the eye will be drawn very powerfully by its *suggestion* of motion. Gradation is perspective created by shading—and we recognize perspective as one of the dynamic forces in art. When the eye is drawn to a space which contains no detail but gradation, the original impulse of the line is continued.

As an agent of light, gradation exhibits its loveliest effects and becomes one of the most interesting and useful elements in picture construction. As a force in balance it may frequently replace detail when added items are unnecessary.

30

"Portrait of Myself When Young" by Ben Shahn. Collection, The Museum of Modern Art, New York.

Balance of principality

or isolation

34. Amidst the mob and turmoil of this scene, the senator at the right, sound asleep, by the strength of his immediate attraction, balances and defines the entire picture.

33. The total isolation of the small figure at the right, far removed from the large foreground group, tells us unquestionably that he is the principal subject. Compare his small weight with that of the girl in Illustration 5, who, despite being the balancing factor, is not the main subject. Note here, however, that the group crosses the middle of the canvas.

"Death of Caesar" by Jean Léon Gérôme.

These qualities are not really synonymous, but they are close enough so that they should be mentioned together. In discussing the principle of the steelyard, we said that a small item could balance a very large one whose position was closer to the fulcrum, because of the increase of weight and importance which isolation gives.

An isolated figure can equate with a group, such as the sleeping senator among the empty benches and pillars in Gérôme's "Death of Caesar." The main group is placed near the middle; the small item at the extreme right. Even Caesar in the foreground—covered by drapery and in half shadow—is less potent as an item of balance than this lone figure.

Balance of cubical space

Since a picture represents depth as well as length and height, this leads to the development of balance in the chain of items that go from foreground to background. There must be a neutral space in the distance to create sufficient attraction to counteract the foreground. Or, there may be an attraction in the foreground that is so strong that it leaves the distance unnoticed. The picture must have balance from front to back or else one section or the other will overpower the whole. This is a more subtle balance than we have seen in vertical and lateral balance. The "aggression" of many foreground items, which may be essential as far as form and value are concerned, is caused by the lack of balancing complements in the back planes of the picture.

One important thing to bear in mind is that balance is not necessarily dependent upon objects of attraction. The very essence of balance is movement from one part of the picture to another. This movement is dictated by arrangement and can often be achieved by *intention* or *suggestion* of movement in a given direction.

35. (*Opposite page, top*) *The strength of the foreground here might easily have overpowered the background and resulted in a complete lack of depth. However, the succession of planes from front to back, both linear and those created by light and dark, result in a balanced cubical space.*

36. (*Opposite page, below*) *Compare with above. Both paintings represent movement from front to back and from side to side. In the Sloan, however, the lateral movement of the figures and the storm-swept trees draw us into the depth of the picture along a different path. In the Bellows, the eye is inclined to zigzag in, and in the Sloan, to sweep elliptically.*

"Blue Morning" by George Bellows. National Gallery of Art, Washington, D.C.   Chester Dale Collection.

"Dust Storm, Fifth Avenue" by John Sloan. The Metropolitan Museum of Art, New York. George A. Hearn Fund.

2. Entrance and Exit

WHILE MYSTERY, SUBTLETY AND EVASIVE CHARM all have their place in a work of art, they should not stand in the way of one necessary quality—IMMEDIATE ATTRACTION. The picture should be like an open door to the viewer without anything blocking the threshold.

Getting into the picture

There must be one spot or area to which the other parts are subordinate and to which the eye is immediately attracted. This, the starting-point for viewing, must be simple and uncluttered and have the essential ingredient of *leading* the eye on further into the picture. Any one element that stops the eye so powerfully that it simply cannot go on is destructive to the composition, and must be carefully avoided.

The picture that you intend to live with must possess qualities that will bear close scrutiny and even analysis. Remember that the actual picture space in nature is somewhat like that of a funnel to the eye. Its size varies according to the extent of the distance that is represented. The eye commands an *angle* of 60 degrees. The *extent of the area* that the eye takes in can be a matter of miles. This extension must always be considered when striving for balance and unity.

Sketch based on John Constable's "Sir Richard Steele's Cottage."

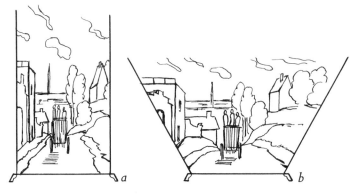

37. a. The focal point of the viewing eye b. The actual area encompassed by the eye covers a 60-degree angle.

34

38. The zigzag of the road draws the eye into the picture immediately. There is no escape from it, and we are led to a central point from which our observation slowly revolves throughout the scene and back to the starting point (see Circular Observation, page 42).

"Road Near L'Estaque" by Georges Braque. Collection, The Museum of Modern Art, New York.

The chief problem that formal balance over a central point presents is that it creates a straddle, or a position akin to landing with a foot on each side of a dividing line when playing hop-scotch. In all pictures of deep perspective the best mode of entry is to *skate* in, with a series of zigzags, since the easiest course for the eye to follow is the line—especially long, receding ones stretching towards us—these are the ones most likely to draw us into the picture. The underlying principle here is that of PERSPECTIVE RECESSION, which is most widely used by the landscape artist whose main subject often lies in the middle distance.

However, when use of lines is impossible, receding spots or accents serve the same purpose. The rule of perspective recession applies not only to scenes but also to portrait or foreground figure pictures. Naturally, if the subject is in the immediate foreground, the eye finds it at once. Even in such pictures, however, the artist

35

39. The figure on horseback attracts immediate attention and the eye continues along his route, curious to see where he is going. After entering the grove of trees, it moves to the distant hills at the left.

must take particular care to avoid all lines, however tiny, that might distract the eye from the subject.

Imagine a seascape with the sea running towards you. Long lines appear in the foreground, but just as in nature, there is a breaking and interlacing of lines in the form of waves. A succession of horizontal lines is, however, the character of a marine picture.

40. Although the subject is immediately recognizable, the large foreground tree acts as a stepping stone into the picture.

41. We enter by joining the group in the foreground and are strongly attracted by the stark, overpowering tree so in contrast to the jollity of the scene. The tree carries us round the entire picture.

"Winter Scene" by Hendrick Avercamp.

Only when the force of these horizontals is broken, either by the sky or by zigzag, angular forms, can the eye come to rest on the subject itself. A great danger of long lines—which are so attractive to the eye—is that they can very easily lead the eye *away* from the subject and right out of the picture.

An excellent example of this is a landscape with a stone wall. The artist can be so taken by the texture and construction of the wall itself that he places it in the foreground. The eye comes upon it, and travels horizontally out of the picture. A more clever and subtle treatment of this subject would be to use the stone wall with all of its interest, as a jumping-off place to get *into* the picture, not *out* of it. How can this be achieved? You can perhaps very carefully paint the foreground slightly out of focus, thus providing an elevation—the wall—not to climb over, but to soar over.

A barrier across the middle distance is almost as objectionable. In a picture of a river embankment the eye comes abruptly against its upper line, which is accented, and from this dives off into the

37

"Christina's World" by Andrew Wyeth. Collection, The Museum of Modern Art, New York.

42. The eye falls without hesitation on the figure in the grass, pursues a course round the swath of cut grass to the barn and then to the house. Compare the balance of elements here with Illustration 10.

fathomless space of the sky, no intermediate object giving a hint of anything existing between that and the horizon.

In order to use such a subject it is necessary to oppose the horizontal of the bank by an item that overlaps and extends above it, as the sail of a boat. If possible, continue this transitional feeling in the sky by cloud forms that carry the eye up. Attraction in the sky creates a depth for penetration which the embankment blocks.

In Turner's "Approach to Venice," (Page F) the gondolas lead us to the subject, and the graceful arch of the sky also presses us towards it. You can easily substitute cattle instead of gondolas, and woods for the spired city; or groups of figures, sheep, rocks, etc. The composition is fundamental, and will accommodate many subjects.

43. A rapid exit through the middle is carefully avoided by the strength of the two balancing spots of interest on either side of the window—the violin case and the dressing table. We pass from one to the other and round the room before stepping on to the balcony.

"Interior with a Violin Case" by Henri Matisse. Collection, The Museum of Modern Art, New York. Lillie P. Bliss Collection.

Getting out of the picture

Getting out of the picture successfully is every bit as important as getting into it. This does not mean, however, *backing* out. Passing through and out is the main objective, but you must create the exit you want. This means avoiding at all costs possible escapes en route and providing a single logical means of leaving the picture.

In portraits, there can be no doubt what the subject is. If the background is blank, the viewer has no choice but to back out of the picture. But suppose, for instance, there is a shadowy curtain in the background which is partly drawn open revealing a glimpse of a landscape beyond. The effect is subtle. It does not disturb the viewer's initial observation of the subject, but when he has completed this, his eye is drawn towards the distance and out. This avoids an abrupt breaking off of contact with the subject.

Any background elements that are introduced into a portrait are balanced round a fulcrum—the subject. The subject becomes part of a scheme, but remains the focus of attention and the central

39

"Half-Length Portrait of a Young Man" by Il Giorgione. Bayer Staatsgemälde-sammlungen, Munich.

44. An excellent way out—through a door, which here is the last object the eye meets after having roved the figure. Its attraction is not so great that we come upon it immediately and its placement allows us to view the entire picture before leaving.

"The Stonecutters" by Gustave Courbet. Deutsche Fotothek, Dresden.

45. Place your hand over the patch of sky on the upper right and see how the picture closes in. This small light area, while not detracting from the subject, leads the eye naturally out of the picture.

40

point about which the other parts are balanced. A patch of sky in a dark background can expand the dimensions of the picture greatly, and also provide a very important sense of atmosphere. Such air holes, or breathing spaces, when well-coordinated do not distract from the subject. Rather, they tend simply to give depth. Beyond this, just the mere variety that they add to the surface excites the eye, which naturally follows from dark to light, and thus is led easily out of the picture.

Just as we enter the picture by means of curves or zigzags, we should leave the same way. The eye should *never* be permitted to leave the principal figure or object and go straight back and out through the middle. If this is allowed, the width of the picture is neglected. Therefore, if the attraction of the natural exit is greater than other objects, there is no valid reason for their existence.

The exit should be so carefully guarded that after the viewer's eye has roamed about and seen everything, it comes upon the exit naturally.

Providing two or more exits is a common error of bad composition. This is the main objection to balance on a central point, which produces two spaces of equal importance on either side.

46. A small bright spot of blue sky above the open door to the left creates a natural exit here, but we do not find it until, having left the main subject, we follow the retreating figure.

"The Provider" by Jean Baptiste Chardin. Service photographique, Chateau de Versailles, France.

41

3. Circular Observation

IF IN NATURE you come upon a scene that is naturally framed, you find yourself gazing first at one object and then at another and finally returning again to the first. In other words, you have found a scene worthy of becoming a picture.

If, on the other hand, you find yourself turning to inspect the whole horizon, you have gone beyond the 60-degree arc that the eye encompasses, and have very definitely *not* found a picture. What you have found is a panorama.

In foreground or figure subjects the same principles apply. The main object is to capture the interest of the observer with the theme which in his mind should unfold *according to the artist's plan.*

"Still Life: The Table" by Georges Braque. National Gallery of Art, Washington, D.C. Chester Dale Collection.

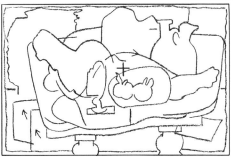

47. Here is a nearly concentric line of observation. If we begin at the focal point, our vision moves in ever-expanding ellipses through the painting.

48. While the basic construction here is pyramidal, note the circular line, which is the path of observation the eye follows upon leaving the main figure. The apex of the pyramid carries us up to the canopy and then round the area of interest.

In "The Slaying of the Unpropitious Messengers," a picture of great power and simplicity of dramatic expression, the vision falls without hesitation on the figure of Pharaoh, easily passing over the three prostrate forms in the immediate foreground. These might have diverted the attention and weakened the subject had not the artist skilfully played them for second place. Their backs have been turned, their faces covered, and, though one to three, the single figure reigns supreme. Note how the figures are made to guide the eye towards him and into the picture. Observe also in the other lines of the picture the artist's intention towards the same end: the staircase, the river, the mountain, the angular contour of the portico tying with the nearer roof projection and making a broken stairway from the left-hand upper corner. Also note how the lines of the canopy compose a special frame for the master figure.

Now, imagine a reconstruction of this composition. Shake the slain messengers into less recumbent and more tragic attitudes, arranged along the foreplane of the picture. Let all the leading lines be reversed. Make them antagonistic to the principles upon which the picture was constructed. The subject indeed will have

43

been preserved and the story illustrated, but the following points will be lost:

- A central dominating point of interest.
- The marked contrast between master and slave.
- The feeling of repose and quiet suggested by a starlit night and the co-ordination of recumbent lines.
- The pathos of the lonely vigil, with the gaze of the single figure strained and fixed upon the distant horizon where he watches for the remnants of his shattered army.

The artist's first conception of this subject was probably that of a pyramid—the head of Pharaoh as the apex and the slaves the base and side lines. The other lines were arranged in part to draw away from this apparent and very common form of composition. The use of concentric lines to draw the viewer from the lower corners of a picture to an apex of a pyramid is a common device of artists.

Here we can easily see an analogy between the simplest form of landscape construction and the foreground or figure subject. The framework of both is the PYRAMID, or what is termed the *structure*

49. In the painting of a single figure or form, the pyramid is a convenient structure upon which to build. Here the pyramidal shape is the central support of the composition—creating a form of formal balance, where the apex of the pyramid falls precisely on a line through the exact middle of the picture.

"The Virgin and Child" by Jan van Eyck. Stadelschen Kunstinstitut, Frankfurt.

44

50. The pyramid as an instrument of perspective. Here it lies flat and provides a strong pull into the picture.

"Marizy-Sainte-Geneviève" by Maurice Utrillo. National Gallery of Art, Washington, D.C.   Chester Dale Collection.

of physical stability. In the landscape the pyramid lies on its side, the apex receding. It is the custom of some figure painters to construct entirely in pyramids, the smaller items of the picture resolving themselves into minor pyramids. In the single figure picture—the portrait, standing or sitting—the pyramidal form destroys the

"The Washerwoman" by Pierre Auguste Renoir. Collection, The Museum of Modern Art, New York. A. Conger Goodyear Fund.

51. As a structural entity, the pyramid is excellent in sculpture. Note the strong unity of form and action here. The eye is so strongly held that it never leaves until it has made a full circuit of the figure.

45

spaces on either side of the figure. Paralleling both the sides and the frame, it leaves long quadrilaterals in place of diminishing segments.

Whether the pyramid is in perspective or on the foreplane of a picture, the principle is: leading lines should carry the eye into the picture or towards the subject.

When reverie begins in a picture, the eye involuntarily makes a circuit of the items presented, starting at the most interesting and widening towards the circumference, as ring follows ring when a stone is thrown into water. The items of a picture may be arranged in elliptical form, and the circuit may bend back into the picture. If the form is described on a vertical plane, the circuit should be there, and if two circuits can be formed the reverie will continue that much longer. The outer circuit finished, the eye may return to the middle again. If in a landscape, for instance, the interest of the sky dominates that of the land, the vision will focus there and come out through the foreground. It is important that the eye

52. Abstract linear design composed of various geometric forms does not completely obscure the pictorial content. Arrangement of balancing and oppositional lines leads the viewer from the steamboat round an elliptical path and back.

"The Steamer 'Odin, II' " by Lyonel Feininger Collection, The Museum of Modern Art, New York. Lillie P. Bliss Bequest.

46

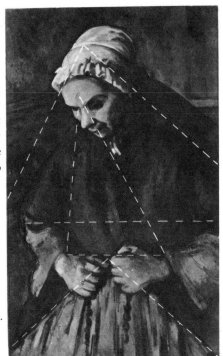

53. A figure constructed almost entirely on a pyramidal form which is used to carry the eye to various items of importance. The basic lowermost pyramid carries us to the focal point of interest —the hands. The apex falls on these over-large hands clenching a rosary, and we immediately understand the significance of the woman's attitude and posture. Thus, we are led from point to point in a vertical ellipse, returning again to the hands.

"La Vieille en Chapelet" by Paul Cézanne. National Gallery, London.

should have this course marked out for it, because left to itself, it might slip away through the sides, and the continuous chain of reverie be broken.

It is interesting to note the cycles in which this great wheel of circular observation revolves, directing the slow revolution of our gaze. In one picture it takes us from the corner of the canvas to the extreme distance and then in a circuit back. In another it moves on a flat plane like an ellipse in perspective. In still another, it first catches the eye in the middle, and unfolds like a spiral.

Much of the painter's attention should be given to keeping his edges so well guarded that the eye in its circuit is kept within the canvas. The large number of changes which an artist makes in his pictures during construction are stimulated by this consideration— how to stop a wayward eye from getting too near the edge and escaping from the picture.

To prove this point, paint a simple black-and-white landscape, with no attempt to create a focus, with no suppression of the corners and no circuit of objects—a landscape in which ground and sky divide the interest equally. Art begins *at that point* and

"A Seaport and Classic Ruins in Italy" by Francesco Guardi. National Gallery of Art, Washington, D.C.   Samuel H. Kress Collection.

54. In this painting, all precautions have been taken to prevent the eye from escaping out of the sides. As we approach each corner, an object or line carries us safely round it until we have completed the entire circuit.

works towards the production of unity, the establishment of a focus, the subordination of parts by the establishment of a scale of relative values, and a continuity of progression from one part to another.

The procedure is as follows:

Decision as to whether the sky or ground shall take precedence.

The production of a central point and a suppression of contiguous parts.

The experimenting with lines which carry the eye away from the focal point and lead it through the picture—a groping for an item, an accent, or something that will attract the eye away from the corner or side of the picture, where, in following the leading lines, it may be brought back towards the focus again.

In the suppression of corners the same instinct for the elliptical line should be followed because the composition, by avoiding the corners, will be described completely within its own space.

48

"The Pottery Seller" by Francisco José de Goya. Museo del Prado, Madrid.

An exceedingly well balanced painting with a basically circular plan of observation and embodying many of the elementary rules of good composition. The use of complementary and analagous colors, as well as lights and darks, provides a balance that is as strong as the form and structure of the picture. Test this painting by applying as many of the principles of composition as you can.

A

"Early Sunday Morning" by Edward Hopper. 1930. Oil on canvas. Collection of the Whitney Museum of Modern Art, New York.

The powerful fundamental horizontal structure of this composition is beautifully balanced by minor vertical forces—the fire hydrant, the barber's pole, and the shadowy mass of the building at the upper right. The upright windows and doorways provide secondary vertical pulls.

B

(Right) Through the use of light from a source outside the picture, the "principality" of the main subject is seemingly obvious. However, the artist, simply by virtue of his position in the foreground, his back to us, emphasizes his importance and counteracts and balances the illuminated subject.

(Below) The principle of the steelyard. The distant craft on the horizon creates a perfect balancing force for the foreground mass. Cover this small boat and note how the picture loses depth. The strong diagonal movement of the boat skilfully cuts the horizontals of sky and water, and provides a natural axis near the middle of the picture— the boy in the stern.

"The Artist's Studio" by Jan Vermeer. New York Graphic Society.

"Breezing Up" by Winslow Homer. National Gallery of Art, Washington, D.C. Gift of the W. L. and May T. Mellon Foundation.

C

"Sunflowers" by Vincent Van Gogh. Philadelphia Museum of Art, Mr. and Mrs. Carroll S. Tyson Collection.

A single unit must relate to the sides of the frame, either by actually touching them or by being united to them in some other way. Here, the vertical sides of the vase are connected to the sides by the line of the table. Notice how the solidity of the smaller element—the vase—is balanced by the lighter but larger mass—the flowers.

D

"Christ Mocked by Soldiers" by Georges Rouault. 1932. Oil on canvas, 36¼ × 28½". Collection, The Museum of Modern Art, New York.

An effective arrangement of three units is achieved through a plan of formal balance— the placement of equal measures on either side of the subject. Note the unifying and balancing strength of the colors, particularly the definition of Christ by the red outline. Compare with Illustration 19 on page 20. **E**

The balancing strength of the delicate vertical masts against the four large horizontal bands is immediately evident. We are led into the picture by way of the foreground gondola which is effectively placed diagonally across the middle and starts us on our reverie.

"Approach to Venice" by Joseph Mallord William Turner.

F

"The Breakfast Room" by Pierre Bonnard. c. 1930–31. Oil on canvas, 63¼ × 44½". Collection, The Museum of Modern Art, New York.

The eye immediately falls on the foreground objects, moves round the table and then to the shadowy figure at the left before taking its natural exit through the window. Note the subtle light-to-dark transition from front to back which creates not only the path of observation, but perspective.

G

"Dutch Interior" by Joan Miró. 1928. Oil on canvas, 36⅛ × 28¾". Collection, The Museum of Modern Art, New York. Mrs. Simon Guggenheim Fund.

Here, balance is achieved through spots and patches of color. Can you, after careful analysis of color and form, find a similarity between this abstract composition and Goya's "Pottery Seller" on Page A?

H

Circular composition

Circular observation in pictures whose structure is *apparently* not circular leads to the consideration of circular composition itself. There is a class of picture in which the intention is to compose under the influence of circular observation—where the circle expresses the first thought in the composition.

It is interesting to note that in this category we find many of what are considered the world's great pictures. Little analysis is necessary to discover this arrangement in most strong compositions.

The head in the "Portrait of Van der Geest" by Van Dyck (Illustration 56) symbolizes the *completeness of the circle*. Like a ring round Saturn, this sphere within the circle is typical of harmony in unity, and for this reason, though it is detached, it has a greater completeness than if joined to a body. It is on this general principle that all circular compositions are based—absorption of attention *within the circuit*.

55. The circular construction here is obvious even to the casual eye. There is no question that the intention was actually to compose round a circle, as the diagram clearly illustrates. Observe the exit that has been carefully provided to allow the eye to leave the confinement of the circular foreground when it is ready.

"Jesus in the House of Mary and Martha" by Tintoretto. Bayer Staatsgemäldesammlungen, Munich.

49

"Cornelius van de Geest" by Sir Anthony Van Dyke. National Gallery, London.

In Tintoretto's "Marriage of Bacchus and Ariadne" (Illustration 7), the floating figure presents us with a shock, even if we consider the time when it was produced. This was a period in art when angels were frequently used throughout a composition simply to fill gaps or create masses. Their postures were dictated by whatever conditions the picture demanded. In this case, the artist needed to complete the circuit begun by the two figures on the ground, so he simply introduced an arc-like figure suspended in air. In addition, the angel fills a space that could otherwise have captured the viewing eye. In the mind of a 16th-century artist these reasons were perfectly valid.

In Watts' "Endymion," the movement of the draperies supplies motion to the figure of Selene, and as a *momentary* action we know

57. The vortex composition—a whirlpool effect, with the fluid movement of the outer circle forming a distinct central cavity. Compare with Illustration 32.

"Endymion" by George Frederic Watts.

50

58. The circle, while not immediately obvious, is the basis of this composition, with the tip of the lace cuffs acting as the focal point. Try carrying the arrows through as many points as possible, making a series of concentric circles and ellipses.

Sketch based on "Arrangement in Grey and Black"
by James A. McNeill Whistler.

it could be possible. However, if the interpretation of motion by hair and drapery were utterly implausible, and the impression, as in the Tintoretto, that of the suspended nude model, few modern painters would use such a figure. It is this touch of realism, even among the transcendental painters, that denotes the clean-cut separations between the modern and mediaeval art sense.

While these two examples show the VORTEX ARRANGEMENT with fluent outlines, Whistler's famous portrait of his mother expresses the same principles in almost rectangular outline. The chairback, the curtain, the framed etching, are all formally placed with respect to the edges of the canvas. We observe them in order, and gradually make a circuit back to the head.

The circle in composition is evident in many pictures where there is no direct evidence that the *intention* was to use it, but where analysis proves that the painter did it naturally.

Review the picture of Whistler's mother through its simple evolution: the head was conceived in its pose, with the next line of interest being the one from neck to feet. This line, besides being the edge of the black mass of the body, is all the more apparent against the light grey wall. But beautiful as it may be, it commits an unlovely act in cutting a picture diagonally, almost from corner to corner. The line is interrupted only by the hands and the handkerchief. Shortly below the knee this is diverted by the baseboard and at the bottom squarely stopped by the solid rectangle of the stool.

Suppose that the picture on the wall were missing; not only would the long parallelogram of the curtain be unrelieved, but the return of the line to the subject in the ensemble of the picture would be broken. This becomes the keystone of the composition.

Now study the vortex arrangement of Meissonier's "1807," with its magnificent sweep of cavalry. The tumultuous energy of one part is balanced by repose in another. Meissonier's composition was expanded after his first conception was nearly completed. It has a horizontal line in the sky and a vertical one through the right end. This slight ridge in the canvas shows the dimensions of his original thought. The added space gave greater opportunity for the manoeuvres of the *cuirassiers*, and set Napoleon to the left of the exact middle, where, by the importance of his figure, he better serves as a balance for the heavier side of the picture.

In the Whistler portrait the keystone was the picture on the wall; in this composition, the group of mounted guardsmen on the left provides a circle's unity and helps to join the middle distance with the foreground. Then by becoming the third point in the triangle, it gives pyramidal solidity to the composition and altogether is quite as important to the picture as the right wing to the army.

59. The vortex arrangement—flowing outer lines from a stable hub, is here conceived on a basically horizontal plan of construction. Study the balancing elements carefully.

"1807" by Jean Louis Meissonier.

Reconstruction for circular observation

There are three forms of composition which produce circular observation:

• Circular composition traceable in what has been first conceived as pyramidal or rectangular.

• Circular composition as the first intention, expressed either on a vertical plane or in perspective, that is, circular or elliptical.

• Composition *made circular*, not by any arrangement of parts, but by sacrifice and elimination of edges and corners.

The value of the circle as a unifying and, consequently, as a simplifying agent cannot be overestimated, especially in solving problems which occur in composition where the circle was not a part of the original scheme, but where its use seems to bring relief to confusion and disorder. In cases where essential items are happily arranged, but as a whole refuse to compose, add some element or readjust a part and see if you can produce circular observation. This will often prove to be the solution.

Just as progression in a straight line will soon carry the eye out of the picture, circular progression keeps it within bound. It follows then that if circular observation is the best means of appreciation, circular composition is the most telling form of presentation.

In order to secure a vortex (central point) bounded by a circle, you can surround a head or figure with flying drapery, a halo or any linear item which serves both to cut out and hem in. To help find the central point, hold your hands as a tunnel before your eye.

In this class of composition the background especially must be made the complement of the subject. What the subject fails to contain the background supplies. The subject, or most interesting part, should lie either *within* the circuit or be the most important item *of* the circle. It should never be *outside* the circle. If it appears there, the eye is thrown off the elliptical track.

A common mistake in use of the circular form is to make it too obvious. There are many pictures in which the formal lines of construction are obvious, such as Sassetta's "The Obsequies of St. Anthony Abbott" (Illustration 60). The formality of the arrangement is on a par with the strain and effort expressed in every one of its figures. The curve of priests seems to tempt you

60 (Above). 61 (Below). Compare these two essentially circular groupings. The Sassetta presents a stiff semi-circle of figures that somehow destroys the emotional nature of the death-bed scene. Rembrandt's circle of figures is a skilful, well-balanced arrangement. Here the harmony of the circle is beautifully displayed.

to push the end man and wait for the others to topple—more to create a rearrangement than any commotion. The fact that the intention of this work is decorative rather than pictorial does not justify a stereotyped representation.

Compare this painting with Rembrandt's etching of "Christ Preaching," in which, though the weight on either side of Christ is about evenly divided, a formal placement has been most carefully avoided. The general impression is merely that the Healer is the focal point of a body of people who surround Him.

A composition in an oval or circle is much more easily achieved than in a rectangular space, as the annoying problem of corners is disposed of. However, these canvases are rarely used, one reason being that galleries and hanging committees find it difficult to arrange them suitably with other representational pictures. Artists attempt in the majority of compositions, however, to fit the picture proper to the fluent lines of the circle or oval.

Keep in mind the cardinal rule of linear composition, that the eye travels the path of least resistance. You will then understand this principle of composition: the various items of a composition are taken at their required value *to the extent to which they adhere to the established plan of observation.*

62. *The painting exhibits an almost perfect plan of circular construction. Like a giant wheel, the entwined figures and horses are ready to rotate at the slightest push.*

"Rape of the Daughters of Leucippis" by Peter Paul Rubens. Bayer Staatsgemäldesammlungen, Munich.

55

63. Count the number of triangular forms in this woodcut—a composition consisting almost entirely of angular forms, relieved only by the circular area created by the arched figure and the round cistern.

"The Fuji Seen Behind a Cistern" by Katsuṣhika Hokusai.

4. Angular Composition

In ANGULAR COMPOSITION the return of the eye over its course, as in circular observation, is practically eliminated. While the circle and ellipse offer a succession of items and events, one the sequence of the other, so that the eye travels like a boomerang, angular composition sends a direct shaft with no return.

The triangle

Here the pleasure of reverie through an endless chain must be exchanged for the stimulation of a shock, for force by concentration, for ruggedness at the expense of elegance. Pure triangular composition is a form rarely seen. In most cases the lines of the triangle are obvious in the first stages, and other lines or points are added to destroy or modify them.

In Daumier's "Return from the Market," the main form is composed of triangles and the supporting spaces are triangles. Such construction is particularly stable, as these focus on the line of interest. Some artists construct most of their pictures in a series of related triangles.

56

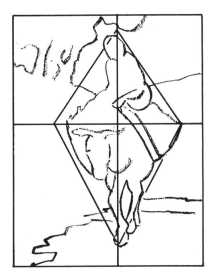

64. Triangular construction on the natural axis. Study the number of subtle triangular forms within the painting, such as the animal's head.

"Return from the Market" by Honoré Daumier.

The vertical line in angular composition

When Giotto was asked for his conception of a perfect building, he produced a circle. When Michelangelo was asked, he designated a cross. Both are excellent bases for good architecture *and* good pictures. If the extremities of the Greek cross are connected by arcs, a circle will result. If the Latin cross is bounded in the same way, a kite shape, or ellipse, emerges. The two designs are in a sense similar. From the pictorial standpoint, they provide the framework by which the same space can be filled. (Illustration 65.)

The simple vertical line is monotonous. Its bi-section produces balance—and a cross is the result. Going further, two crosses

57

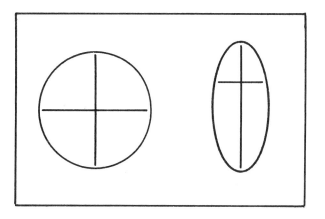

65. A basis for construction—the cross. The Greek cross at left when bounded forms a circle; the Latin cross, an ellipse.

placed together, arms touching, and three crosses in a similar position, will represent the picture plan of the grouping so frequently used by Raphael: a central figure balanced by another on each side, the horizon joining them, and behind this the balance repeated in trees and other figures.

Pictorially, the vertical line is much more important than any other. In nature, it is the direction of gravity. It distinguishes upright man from the lower animals. It also can stand alone, while

66. The cross itself is here repeated in the arrangement of the figures.

"Descent from the Cross" by Rogier van der Weyden.

67. *The strength of vertical lines is heightened when they are bisected. This series of crosses creates a carefully balanced composition, and, although pictorial content is sublimated, presents a pleasing effect. The actual structural form and pattern take precedence in most of Mondrian's work.*

68. *The verticality of the figures, symbolizing their staunch upright characters, is accented by the erect pitchfork and repeated in the board-and-batten house. However, a necessary balancing horizontal—the porch roof— strongly bisects those heavy vertical elements, acting as an anchor to keep the whole composition from soaring straight up into the air.*

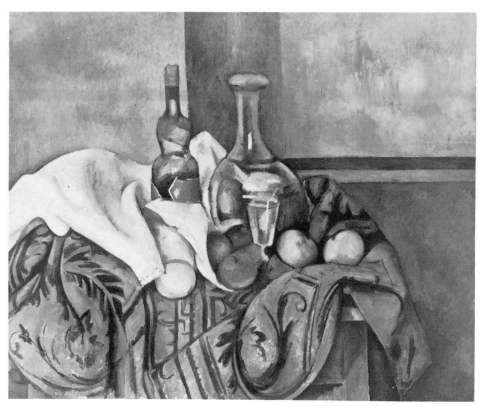

"Still Life" by Paul Cézanne. National Gallery of Art, Washington, D.C.

69. In this still life, the power of a vertical is plain. The eye immediately falls on the wine bottle and decanter which nearly alone balance the mass of the draped cloth and fruit.

all other lines demand supports. Of two lines of equal force the vertical is the one first seen. In composition, therefore, it takes precedence.

Start with a subject represented by a vertical line—a tree or figure. The directness, rigidity, isolation and unqualified force of such a line demands balance. If you visualize a frame or put sides on the picture, you will see why a horizontal line bisecting the vertical becomes necessary. Length and breadth must be represented, something in two dimensions started, and so the four sides of a frame are essential.

In sculpture this consideration is unimportant. A statue is framed by air. The vertical of a single figure always pierces the atmosphere, and the sculptor's only consideration is for the mass to look right from any point of view. In Carpeaux' "The Dance," the picturesque group of figures would easily fit a frame, because the

60

vertical figure in it is supported by horizontals—not only actual lines, but a *feeling* of lateral movement. This piece of sculpture is a cross within a cylinder, but the principle is just as forcible on a flat plane.

"The Crucifixion" by Morot is more dramatic than picturesque, and more effective unencumbered by the limitations of a frame. The presence of the frame creates three empty spaces, one above the horizontal and one on either side of the vertical. Therefore, although the single idea of the dying Saviour is strong enough to justify isolation, it does not unite with anything else within the compass of vision. Therefore, it does not compose with its frame.

"The Dance" by Jean Baptiste Carpeaux.
Façade, Opéra, Paris.

"The Crucifixion" by Matthias Grünewald.
Isenheim Altar.

70 (Left). 71 (Right) Two examples of the use of the crossed vertical. The sculpture has greater unity of form and balance within itself. The painting would be better off without a frame—here the cross is not self-contained, but tends to extend indefinitely beyond the limits of the frame.

61

72. Verticals unopposed by horizontals cut the picture into three separate areas, and destroy pictorial unity.

In the composition of the "Beautiful Gate" by Raphael, the two pillars destroy all chance for unity by spanning the whole distance from bottom to top. Three pictures result instead of one—an elaborately framed triptych. Even with these verticals cutting the picture into sections, some of the necessary unity of pictorial structure could have been achieved if horizontals had been introduced between them and in front, or even behind. There is

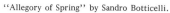

73. Another example of lack of structural unity. Compare with Illustration 72.

62

no structural connection between the several parts. The impulse to exhibit the wonderful columns in their remarkable perfection of detail caused the picture as a whole to be sacrificed.

The "Allegory of Spring" by Botticelli is an example of structure lacking both circular cohesion and the stability of cross adhesion— it might be extended indefinitely on either side or cut into four separate panels. The accessories of the figures offer no help towards union. Apparently no effort was made even in the original conception of the subject towards attaining structural unity. Each figure or group is self-sufficient, and the whole represents a collection of separate ideas. This is not composition, but addition.

What of the single figure in standing portraiture? Only the person is presented, and there is no thought but that of personality. The outline stands relieved by spaces of nothingness. Though less apparent in this, the principle of union with the sides still applies. What is known as a "lost and found outline" applies here—the artist tries to make the background homogeneous with the vertical mass, to make the line give way so that the surrounding tone may be let in. Such is the feeling in many of the most subtle of Whistler's portraits.

74. The verticalness of this figure is cleverly attached to the frame by the arms and by the blending of the upper background with the tones of the figure.

"Little Rose of Lyme Regis" by James A. McNeill Whistler.
Museum of Fine Arts, Boston.

"A Windmill by a River" by Jan van Goyen. National Gallery, London.

75. In landscapes, the first line of construction is most often the horizontal. Here, the unending expanse of sky and land is effectively pierced by the small dramatic upright of the windmill, which gives the picture scale and definition within the frame of the sides.

Angular composition

based on the horizontal

Just as the vertical may be called the figure painter's line, the horizontal is the landscape painter's line. Pictures are made by building upon and round these basic lines. We have noted briefly the devices which aid the figure painter in his use of one or many verticals. To consider the horizontal, go out-of-doors to earth and sky, where nature constructs on surfaces that follow the horizon.

The composition problem is the same with each of these lines and the principle governing the solution is identical—balance by equalization of forces. *When a line coincides with only one side of the picture, it becomes necessary to cross it with an opposing line.* The rec-

64

"Windmill of Wijk" by Jacob van Ruisdael. Rijks Museum, Amsterdam.

76 (Above). 77 (Below) Compare the use of the basic horizontal structures of these two paintings. Both achieve a balance of line and mass effectively, and to some extent similarly. Make a line diagram of the Motherwell and see if you can find parallels with the Ruisdael.

"The Voyage" by Robert Motherwell. Collection, The Museum of Modern Art, New York. Gift of Mrs. John D. Rockefeller, 3rd.

tangular cross is not the only means of attaining this—the crossing of lines *at a long angle* is equally effective. A series of right angles will in time arrive at the same point as a tangent, but less quickly. While each angle in such a pattern produces an equality between horizontal and vertical, the tangent expresses their synthesis.

Once a line passes through the first (or necessary) line of construction, either the horizontal or vertical, it incorporates itself into the picture. What it becomes thereafter is of no great importance. The real importance of a line occurs only at the moment it passes through the main line of construction. If you make simple line diagrams of a few masterpieces, this point will become clear. You will find that such diagrams represent either the actual lines of direction (or lines of suggestion) from point to point or mass to mass and will comfortably fill the four sides of the frame *as a linear design*.

78. The vertical columns here bisect the picture, preventing structural unity. The only unifying factor is the attitude of the two figures, which, however, is lacking in Illustration 72, a similar construction.

"The Annunciation" by Fra Angelico. Diocesan Museum, Cortona, Italy.

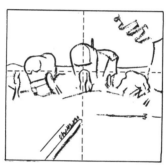

79. The use of diagonals to disrupt a strongly horizontal composition. The tops of the wagons cross the canvas diagonally into the exact vertical axial line which is strongly accented by the rear of the horse and the wagon. The extreme flatness of earth and sky are perfectly balanced by this angular grouping.

The first step in analyzing pictures is finding the first or most commanding and necessary line. After you find this thread, the whole composition will unravel and a reason for each stitch will be disclosed.

Take a horizontal baseline with verticals erected from it, but not crossing it. No picture results because there is no cross. Such a design is found in many of Fra Angelico's paintings of saints and angels. An example of this is "The Annunciation of the Virgin," which is not pictorial nor a composition from the picture point of view. Its homogeneity depends not on interchange of line or upon other mechanics of composition, but only upon a unity of associated ideas. In instances where some of the figures are *joined* by horizontal lines or masses that bisect verticals, the pictorial intention can be felt.

67

Sketches based on landscapes by Henry Ranger.

80. Here the overpowering horizontals, in their massiveness, prove too much for the tiny opposing verticals of the masts.

81. Notice how the strong horizontal of the stone wall, reflected in the base of the tree line, cuts the picture sharply in two. The trees in their stark verticality provide the necessary balancing elements. However perfectly balanced, there is a lack of interest.

Illustration 80 showing a shore with overhanging clouds has a persistent number of horizontals. Nothing but the lighthouse and the masts of the vessels serve for counter-active lines. Because of their great distance, they would do little to relieve the disparity of line were it not for the aid of the vertical pillar of cloud and the pull downwards which the eye receives in the pool below the shore. The most troublesome line in this picture is the shoreline, but an effort has been made here to break its monotony by the accents of bushes on either side. What at first seems to be a composition "going all one way," displays after analysis a strong attempt towards use of the principle of crossed lines.

In the woods picture (Illustration 81), the stone wall is the damaging line. Not only does it parallel the bottom line (always unfortunate) but it cuts the picture in two from side to side. The

68

bottom line of the distant woods provides another parallel running the full length of the picture. The verticals, however, weaken the horizontals until there is an almost perfect balance, as the crossing lines weigh out evenly.

The sketch of Claude Lorraine's from "The Book of Truth" shows a great left-angle composition of line which is not very satisfactory, because of the lack of weight of the long arm of the "steelyard." However, the principle here is correct, and the composition could be balanced easily by the addition of some small item of interest to the extreme left. It is not, however, a commendable type of composition, although the plan of lines is excellent. If the whole composition were pushed to the left, the open spaces would at once be relieved.

The principle of the diagonal being equivalent as a space filler to the crossed horizontal and vertical is shown by comparison of Illustration 81 with Illustration 79 on page 67, in which the fore-

"Sketch from the Book of Truth" by Claude Lorraine.

82. The whole composition is massed on one side of the canvas. The horizontal of the land is balanced by the strong vertical tree to form a right angle. If the tree did not completely fill the right side, some small balancing force would have to be introduced on the left.

69

ground has been treated this way. The force of a horizontal is more cleverly weakened by such a line. Besides adding variety, it accomplishes its intention with less effort.

The sky is but one of two major elements in landscapes and in most cases it is secondary. If the sky is to blend with an interesting landscape it must take a back seat. If it causes divided interest, its intensity must be sacrificed. Drawings, photographs and color sketches of skies can be studied with the intention of combining them with landscapes but keep in mind when fitting them to the linear scheme of landscape that they must have only secondary interest.

Skies that move away from the horizon diagonally suggest oppositional feeling, and belong in every artist's portfolio. They are more effective than a series of clouds, the bottoms of which parallel the horizon, especially when these float isolated in the sky. When a formal terrace of clouds entirely fills the sky space, this massive structure is felt more than horizontal lines, just as a series of closely parallelled lines blends together.

"Ballet Scene" by Edgar Degas. National Gallery of Art, Washington, D.C.

83. The force of a diagonal is here apparent. Besides adding perspective, it acts as the oppositional force to the verticality of the figures in a more interesting way than would a horizontal.

70

"The Carrying of the Cross" by Hieronymus Bosch.

84. A composition based on a diagonal construction—here symbolic of the theme— the cross.

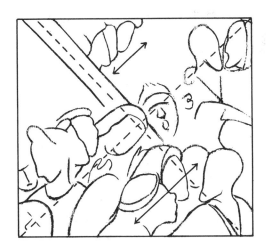

Line of beauty

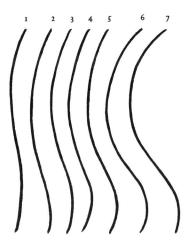

"Torso of Ile de France" by Aristide Maillol. The Metropolitan Museum of Art, New York. Edith Perry Chapman Fund. Photo courtesy of The Museum of Modern Art, New York.

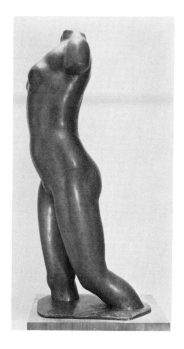

85. William Hogarth's series of seven curves. Compare No. 4 with Maillol's "Torso" at right.

The most elastic and variable of the fundamental forms of composition is the so-called "line of beauty" as found in the letter "S," or angularly in the letter "Z." This form is particularly adapted to upright arrangements. You can trace this curvilinear feeling through many of the great figure compositions of the Renaissance.

In Hogarth's essay on "The Line of Beauty," he set forth a series of seven curves, selecting No. 4 as the most perfect. This is duplicated in nature by the line of a woman's back. If two such curves

86. Find "The Line of Beauty" here that corresponds to that shown in Illustration 87.

"Reclining Nude" by Auguste Renoir. Collection, The Museum of Modern Art, New York. Gift of Mr. and Mrs. Paul Rosenberg.

72

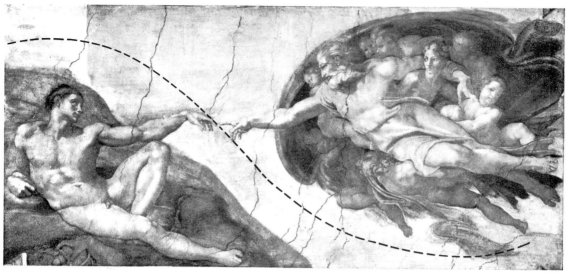

87. The curvilinear "S" forms a perfect balance of elements and imparts movement and life, which is here the essence of the subject.

are joined side by side, they produce the beautiful curve of a mouth or Cupid's bow. Horizontally, the line is very serviceable in landscape. As a vertical, it is like the upward sweep of a flame which, ever-moving, is symbolic of activity and life. To express this line both in the composition of the single figure and of many figures was the constant effort of Michelangelo.

The compound curve containing the "S" line has perfect balance, and can easily be created in the standing figure. It has an element of grace, and affords the same delight as the interweaving curves of a dance or the fascinating spirals of wafting smoke. Classic landscapes in which many elements are introduced (or any subjects in which scattered elements are to be swept together) are controlled and dependent upon this principle. An absolute line is not a necessity, but points of attraction which the eye can easily follow are essential. Many simple subjects owe their force and distinction entirely to a bold sweeping curved line.

However, when a subject demands a rugged form, you might exchange the sinuous line for an abrupt and forcible zigzag. In such an arrangement, the eye is pulled sharply across spaces from one object to another, if the space itself contains little of interest.

When painting skies, artists often use film-like cirrus clouds as

73

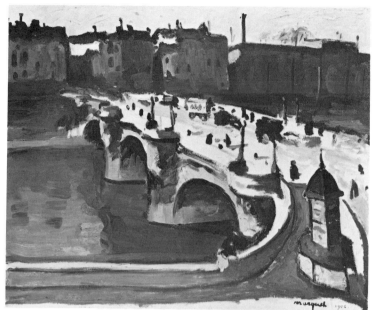

88. The sweep of the curved horizontal line of the parapet draws the two parts of the scene together, acting in a transitional sense, as well as a balancing one.

"The Pont Neuf" by Albert Marquet. National Gallery of Art, Washington, D.C. Chester Dale Collection.

the background to the stronger forms of the cumulus, in order to create oppositional feeling. Besides strengthening the structure pictorially such an arrangement frequently imparts great swing and movement in the lines of a sky, carrying the eye away from the horizon. When you want positive cloud motion, use oppositional masses that are suggestive of wind, with the different strata showing contrasted action of air currents.

The "line of beauty" may be used in any form of composition.

Structural line

A structural line exists in the initial form of every picture, and conjunctive lines join naturally to such a form. These two types of line are the concern of the scientific artist.

Line has a distinct aesthetic value. Pictures conceived in vertical lines convey dignity, solemnity and serenity—pillars, trees with straight trunks, ascending smoke, etc. A series of horizontals affects the viewer with only slightly less force.

But when the line slants and ceases to support itself, or becomes curved, this suggests movement and evokes another set of emotions. Zigzags typify the quick darting movement of lightning. The vertical curved line is emblematic of the tongue of flame and the horizontal curve of a gliding serpent. In the circle and ellipse,

74

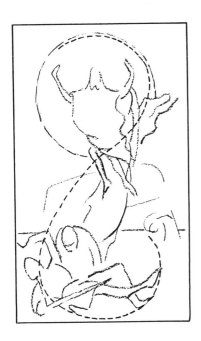

89. The vertical structural line here is actually an "S" as can be seen in the diagram. This line strongly symbolizes emotion, and visually suggests the mystic resurrection as well as the physical upward movement involved. Note the cross within a circle formed by the Christ figure.

"The Resurrection" by Matthias Grünewald. Isenheim Altar.

we feel the whirl and fascination of continuity. The linear impulse in composition therefore plays a part in emotional art independent of the subject.

Painters are rarely governed by a positive linear form in their first conceptions. The outlines of great compositions only hint at, but give no visible evidence of, planned linear design. The requirement of linear design to fill a space beautifully is solved in pictorial composition by the ways in which the artist *adds* to the fundamental construction those items whose outlines connect with the frame.

5. Composition with One
or More Units

A SINGLE IDEA represented by a single unit—for example, a figure —causes the frame or canvas circumference itself to become a matter of serious concern to the artist.

To unify a unit by enclosing it within four sides with those sides can only be accomplished in two ways: either by having the

90. The single figure presents a difficult problem to the artist—that of unity within a frame. One solution is to connect the actual mass to the sides, here admirably and subtly accomplished. The woman is diagonally placed and lightly touches one side with her elbow while being firmly anchored to the other by the large mass of her skirt.

"Anna Zborowska" by Amedeo Modigliani. Collection, The Museum of Modern Art, New York. Lillie P. Bliss Collection.

76

91. *Another means of tying the vertical single figure to the sides. Here a line— the edge of the grass—actually connects the child to the sides. Her foot touches another line at the bottom and her head enters the edge of the flower bed at the top.*

"A Girl with a Watering Can" by (Pierre) Auguste Renoir. National Gallery of Art, Washington, D.C. Chester Dale Collection.

mass of the figure touch the sides of the canvas or stretch towards them. The unit maintains its stability amid its surroundings in proportion to the strength or number of such points.

When a single figure stands within the frame and no contact can occur, the background should contain an oppositional mass or line that attaches the vertical sides of the figure to the sides of the canvas at some point. A gradation would be equivalent to such a line—often the shadow from the figure serves this purpose. If the shadow that unites the outline with the background subdues or destroys this outline, the attachment becomes stronger. At the same time the positive outline on the light (unshaded) side finds contrast and balance in the area of shade and mystery.

Some knowledge of CHIAROSCURO, a style of pictorial art using only light and shade, is a necessity for achieving pictorial unity of the single figure. (See Illustration 92.)

Some artists seem to feel that the purpose of the portrait is to present an impression of a personality and therefore should contain nothing else. They feel that the background is something that should not be seen, and they spend more effort in painting a space with

77

92. Pictorial unity of the single figure is effectively achieved through the use of "chiaroscuro" —light and shade. Gradation fulfils the same purpose as line.

"Portrait of Walt Whitman" by Thomas Eakins.
The Pennsylvania Academy of the Fine Arts.

nothing in it than in putting something in that may not be seen. In the process they create a space that says a great deal it should not.

Two units

Nothing is more difficult than the composition of two units, especially when both are of equal importance. One must dominate —either in size or attraction, feeling or action. You can find examples of two equal figures on the same canvas, but pictorially they lack the essential of complete art—unity.

The foreplacement of one figure over another does not always give it prominence. Light as an element is stronger than position. Of two subjects, one may have precedence of place and one of lighting.

A major difficulty in the arrangement of two units is uniting them. If, for instance, they are opposed in feeling as strongly as two fencers, the union must be secured in the background. Perspective settles most of the difficulty.

Sacrifice is the greatest contributing force to contrast—the more important subject is made obvious by what is conceded to it.

78

93. (Left) The use of both light and position gives the young girl prominence; however, the duenna's shadowy figure, plus her self-conscious attitude brings her to a status of some importance in the composition. She is in the background but not obscure and acts as a balancing measure for the obvious weight of the girl.

"A Girl and her Duenna" by Bartolome Esteban Murillo. National Gallery of Art, Washington. D.C.   Widener Collection.

94. (Right) A quite different situation from above. Both figures are of equal importance. They are united by the lines of the banquette and the table. The foreplacement of the woman at the right is balanced by the direct stare of the one at the left. Their heads and faces are their strongest contrasting elements.

"Café du Dôme" by Guy Pène du Bois. National Gallery of Art, Washington, D.C. Gift of Chester Dale.

Three units

In the combination of three units the objection of formal balance disappears. If one unit is opposed by two, the force gained by the one through isolation is equal to the other two. In such an arrangement the two may be united by overlapping so that, although the sense and idea of two is present, it is shown in one mass as a pictorial unit. This seems to offer the best solution.

Other good forms are two separated units joined by other items and opposed to one, or the three units joined either directly or by suggestion, balanced like a triangle by opposition.

79

"Chess Players" by Thomas Eakins. The Metropolitan Museum of Art, New York. Gift of the Artist.

95. One of the most effective arrangements for three units—the pyramid. The entire outline of multi-unit constructions must be a first consideration. Random placement creates disharmony and lack of focus of interest.

96. An interesting treatment of three units wherein the two largest are united by the third and smallest, creating pictorial unity simply and naturally. Here the unifying element —the child— is symbolic of the unity of the family.

"Family Group" by Henry Moore. Collection, The Museum of Modern Art, New York. A. Conger Goodyear Fund.

"The Potato Eaters" by Vincent van Gogh. Collection, The Museum of Modern Art, New York. Gift of Mr. and Mrs. A. A. Rosen.

97. One of the most effective group arrangements is to place the figures in an oval. The light and the table are the focal points for this scene.

Groups

In all groups, the outline or shape is important because the figures or units are usually seen against a background of wall or sky, frequently in silhouette. Any fault in contour of the mass is therefore emphasized.

Personality is the first requirement for groups, but harmony of arrangement and picturesqueness are likewise essential. The two best shapes are the oval and the pyramid. Both of these outlines allow a focal point to be established—and this is important. In forming such an arrangement, set the focus first, then add item after item. The final shape will be determined naturally as your group develops.

To obtain a more artistic combination of figures try separation into one large and one small group. Place the principal figure in either. If in the large unit, the figures of the smaller group must

"The Musicians" by Michelangelo Merisi da Caravaggio. The Metropolitan Museum of Art, New York. Rogers Fund.

98. The circular grouping of the three figures on the right is balanced by the fourth, at left, who by his isolation and attitude adds variety to the arrangement.

be sacrificed to this figure, either in pose or lighting. If the principal figure is placed in the smaller group or entirely separate, this isolation will prove sufficient for the distinction.

For a purely artistic composition, the curvilinear S-shape is a good line to build upon. If the curve becomes too obvious, a single oppositional figure will relieve its formality.

Consider the possibilities of keeping a single figure as a reserve, to be placed at the last moment where something is necessary. If the group is too formal in either outline, lateral arrangement or

99. Two groups flank the old musician, but he is really part of the larger group of children, and the pair at the right are thus sacrificed. Note that they are less defined than the other figures, but by their attitude are very much a part of the scene.

"The Old Musician" by Edouard Manet. The National Gallery of Art, Washington, D.C. Chester Dale Collection.

"The Night Watch" by Rembrandt van Rijn. Detail. Rijks Museum, Amsterdam.

100. One of Rembrandt's great group portraits and one of his last. Note the variety of attitudes, postures, and placements. This scene of confusion is heightened by the diversity of its component parts. There is no apparent focal point of attraction.

expression, the reserve figure may be played as a foil to create a diversion.

In all successful group paintings the principle of sacrifice has been employed. Rembrandt was one of the first painters to discover this. When the order to paint the "Municipal Guard" (commonly known as "The Night Watch") came to him, he saw in it an opportunity to indulge some ideas he had about the pictorial. Knowing what this entailed, he persevered, despite the mutterings of his sitters, the majority of whom were ill-pleased with where he had placed them. When finally the canvas was finished, it was full of mystery, suggestiveness and subtle qualities—rare then in Dutch art. Those who had given him the order expressed their opinion of his work by giving a commission to a rival to paint the same group again. This was the end of Rembrandt's career as a painter of portraits. He painted only one canvas of an important group after that—the "Syndics" (Illustration 31).

83

There was actually some good reason for the commissioners' feelings. The composition is a collection of separated individuals, unnecessarily scattered, with placements arbitrary, though through the radial lines of pikes and flagpole the scattered parts are drawn together. This composition reflects the confusion of the scene, yet Rembrandt considered the comparative values as he measured his sitters.

Giving principality to an important figure may be attained by attraction of light (such as a white dress), or by placing the figure at the focus of leading lines (which might be supplied by the architecture of a building), or at the focus of lines created by surrounding figures that proceed towards the principal one, or by including the main figure in the most important line. Also, the principal figure may be the only one in a group who exhibits unconcern or absolute repose, the others by expression or action acknowledging his sovereignty.

In most groups there is an active and a passive element, and many figures are required to play second to a few. The active

101. The central figure in this grouping could not be more obvious. Within the elliptical arrangement, all the attention is focussed on the figure in the light shirt with his arms upraised. The light shines on him, the guns are pointed at him, and his friends cling to him.

"The Third of May" by Francisco José de Goya. Museo del Prado, Madrid.

84

102. An obvious example of the sacrifice of many to the principal figure. Here, all attention is drawn to the figure of Christ—by the supplicant on her knees, the pointing finger on the right and by the over-large and agony-distorted body of Christ, so in contrast to the other figures.

principle is represented by those to whom a single idea is delivered for expression.

In a religious group, where the idea of adoration is paramount, the principal figure is usually, though not always, given a position in the upper part of the picture towards which by gestures, leading lines or directed vision our attention is drawn at once. Note the figures which sacrifice to this effect in "The Crucifixion," by Grunewald.

Here are three general types of group composition:

• Where the interest is focussed upon an object or idea within the picture as in Goya's "Third of May."

• Where the attraction lies outside the picture as in the "Syndics" or "The Night Watch."

• Where absolute repose is expressed and a feeling of reverie dominates the group, as in Caravaggio's "Musicians" (Illustration 98).

The figure in landscape

The vastness of a scene is greatly strengthened by the presence of a lone figure. The panoramic grandeur of the sky attracts us the more if it has also appealed to a figure in the picture. There are many and sufficient reasons why the figure should be included. The figure can be moved about as the fixed conditions of topography demand. Many landscapes would be entirely ineffective without such an element.

Take for example a picture in which lines are parallelling one another in their recession from the foreground or where there is a monotony in a horizontal sequence. The vertical of the figure balances these. The principle is one we already noted: action to balance action in contrary or opposing directions.

The danger of the figure in landscape is that so often it seems to be just dragged in. For the artist there is no painting where the "fitness" of things is more mandatory than in associating figures with landscape.

A fault in construction can frequently be seen in lack of simplicity of foreplane and background. You must determine whether the picture is to be a landscape with figures or figures in a landscape.

The most useful material one can collect in sketching landscapes are positions which will play second or third parts in composition. Sketch cattle or other animals in back or three-quarter view which you can use readily to unite with and lead to their principals.

The main object always has the most attraction. This usually follows without thought. Its presence becomes known because it is so interesting. Figures which are less interesting, which will combine with the subject proper, are what artists long for. Those things which are not of sufficient interest to be worthwhile in themselves are, owing to their lesser significance, of the utmost importance to the main subject.

Note the degree of restraint expressed in most of the figures *successfully* introduced into landscape.

103 (Above). 104 (Below) Compare the use of the figures in these two landscapes. Above, the tiny figures seem to be introduced to give scale to the overpowering elements of nature. Below, the solitary figure is the focal point of the scene, and the elements of the composition are balanced round it.

87

6. Light and Shade

Light is gained through sacrifice of light. In an empty outline, an effect of light is produced by adding darks. We get light in the composition of simple elements by sacrificing one or more elements

"Toilers of the Sea," by Albert Pinkham Ryder. The Metropolitan Museum of Art, New York. George A. Hearn Fund, 1915.

105. A composition almost entirely conceived in light and dark balancing elements.

106. Vermeer used here, as in many of his paintings, an actual light source, such as a window. The light and dark areas are beautifully balanced, but at no time do the shaded areas fall into obscurity.

"The Cook" by Jan Vermeer. Rijks Museum, Amsterdam.

(even a mass) to the demands of the lighter parts. A low-toned and much-tinted white may be made brilliant by dark opposition.

The study of light and dark in composition has the name *chiaroscuro*—in Italian literally "obscure light." We found that line and mass composition strive for balance over a central vertical line. Light and shade is best understood as striving for balance over a broad middle tint. The MEDIUM TONE is the most important, both for tint and color. This controls the distribution of measures in both directions: towards light and towards dark.

Drawings in outline on tinted paper take on a surprising finish when a few darks are added for shadow and the highlights touched in with chalk. The method of working in opaque water-color over a paper tinted to correspond to the general tone of the subject, had its origin in the early art of the Venetian painters. A blue-grey paper was used for a blue day, a yellow paper for a mellow day. Pictorially, the light is more attractive than the dark, but the dark

89

"Christ Among the Children" by Emil Nolde. Collection, Museum of Modern Art, New York. Gift of Dr. W. R. Valentiner.

107. Distribution of light and dark measures are here governed to some extent by the content. The children form the light elements—the other figures sacrificing to them. Christ, however, the central figure, is conceived in a medial tone—his size and position opposing the great light of the children.

108. This lithograph points up the effectiveness of black and white in conveying drama and atmosphere.

"Dempsey and Firpo" by George Bellows. Collection, The Museum of Modern Art, New York. Abby Aldrich Rockefeller Purchase Fund.

109. *An exciting effect achieved with ink and wash. The brilliance of the lesser areas of light is heightened by the greater strength of the darks. Notice the strength of attraction of the small bright surface of the top hat on the driver. We can feel the rain and see it splashing in the gutter.*

"In the Rain" by Childe Hassam. National Gallery of Art, Washington, D.C. Chester Dale Collection.

in isolation is nearly as powerful. With this simple rule the artist can proceed upon a "checker-board," opposing force against force.

As for brilliancy of light, with which painting is concerned, the effect is greater when a small measure of light is opposed to a large measure of dark, than when great light is opposed to little dark. In those cases where much light and little dark produces great brilliance, it is usually because of *gradation* in the light, which gives it a cumulative power. Take receding objects on a foggy day. A small added dark will intensify the light, not only by contrast in measure, but in showing the high color key of the light. When a work deals with a medium tone and darks, with few highlights, the latter gain so much importance as to control the important items.

The middle tones, when *not* used as the undertone of a picture, balance and distribute the lights and darks of objects. When three degrees of tone are used, if the black and white are brought together and the middle tone opposed, a sense of harmony results. The black and white, if mixed, would become a middle tone.

An accent is never more forcible than its intensity, divided by the area it occupies. Take for instance a pen-and-ink sketch of a misty morning. The whole landscape is produced by a small drop of ink spread with a brush in light gradations upon an area 10 × 14 inches. An object in the foreground is inked only 1 × 2 inches

110. Compare the use of the reflected light here with the direct light in Illustration 106. Here the dying rays of the sun strike the whitewashed wall and form a background against which the action is silhouetted. A small trickle of light points to the dog at the bottom. (Note the basic circular plan of construction.)

"The Drinkers" by Honoré Daumier. The Metropolitan Museum of Art, New York. Bequest of Margaret S. Lewisohn, 1954.

in area, but this same amount of black in that small area will possess much more powerful attraction. The rule is: As the area expands, it is balanced by a loss in intensity. To give less attraction to an object, increase the intensity of the surrounding tint or increase its area without increasing its intensity.

From a decorative point of view alone, a picture surface contains the greatest amount of beauty when it is varied by many tones, or by a few *in strong contrast*. Decorative designs have the strongest appeal where the balancing measures are well defined. Schemes with much dark and little light, or much light and little dark, are no more attractive than even division, if in each case a balance of light and dark is sustained. When there is little dark, its accenting power is enhanced. When little light is allowed, it, in the same way, gains in attraction.

When the artist begins a picture, he should first decide on a scheme of light and shade. The direction or source of the light can help in reaching a decision.

These same principles apply to landscape painting. Try to select and produce three, four or five distinct and separate tones in every study. When a beginner's work out-of-doors is incoherent, this is largely because the work has a great number of unimportant planes, a fault resulting from lack of observation of detail instead of large shapes. For this reason, subjects having little or no detail are the best choice. Start with sky and land alone, as they allow for a dynamic line and an interesting division of light and shade. Open, rolling country where the woodland is grouped in masses, is a popular subject.

Principality

The sacrifice of many measures to one is often wisest. The sun setting over fields or through trees might cover but a limited section of the canvas, but it is what we see and remember. The remaining space takes a subordinate role.

Remember that the aim of the artist is to secure light *in the degree* which his subject demands. There are many degrees of light and they must not be confused. A window on the north side will not necessarily bring sunlight into a room to fall upon a posed figure. The fault of many paintings is that the natural conditions are violated and the *exact degree* of illumination which the subject demands is not pictured.

There may be a greater feeling of light in a figure sitting in a shadow than in the same figure next to a window. To the painter,

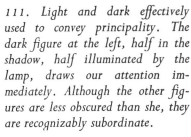

111. Light and dark effectively used to convey principality. The dark figure at the left, half in the shadow, half illuminated by the lamp, draws our attention immediately. Although the other figures are less obscured than she, they are recognizably subordinate.

"The Visit" by Edouard Vuillard. National Gallery of Art, Washington, D.C. Chester Dale Collection.

light and air are only degrees of the same idea. If the figure seated in the shadow is receiving reflected lights, it picks up part of the scheme of brilliant lighting as much as if it were in direct light. The purpose of using shadow is first to accentuate the light, second to secure concentration, third to eliminate unnecessary space and to suggest air and relief by gradation, which every shadow must have.

The Japanese concept of light and dark, *Notan*, differs from this in intent. It merely sets forth an agreeable interchange of light, dark and medium-toned spaces. The great value of this concept, however, should be recognized. In formulating a scheme of light and shade for any picture, light and dark masses should be so arranged as to suggest much of the beauty which flat translation by Notan would yield. A helpful habit is to lay out the flat light and dark scheme of every picture which is to be finished in full relief.

Gradation

Most good pictures are produced in the medium tonal range. A series of gradations in which a graceful flow of line and tone is blended with a forcible stroke will result in a combination of subtlety and strength.

There are three forms of this gradation:

• That in which light shows a gradual diminution of power, as seen upon a wall near a window, or in white smoke issuing from a funnel.

• That in which the color or force of objects weakens as they recede, as in fog.

• That in which the arrangement secures, in disconnected objects, a regular succession of graded measures.

In each case, the pictorial value of gradation is apparent. The landscape painter avails himself of gradation as the figure painter does of his background trappings, counting on cloud shadow to temper *and* unite disjointed items of his picture. He makes use of shading where leading lines are lacking or are undesirable, or to give an additional accent to light by shaded contrast, or to introduce a note of dark by suppressing the tone of an isolated object.

The introduction of a shadow through the foreground or middle

"Moonlight" by Edvard Munch.
Collection, The Museum of
Modern Art, New York.

*112. The shadowy figure, by virtue of remaining untouched by the brilliant light,
more powerfully conveys his isolation and gloom. Notice how completely he is
incorporated into the surrounding shadow by both tone and line.*

distance, over which the eye travels to the light beyond, gives
great depth. Another device in landscape painting is to attain light
by the use of a graded scale of contrasts. A cumulative gradation
which suddenly stops has the same force in light and shade as a long
line which suddenly changes into a short line of opposed direction.
They are only to be employed where there is something important
to follow.

It is not enough that pictures have lights and darks, however.
Balance is quite as important as line and degree. The proportion of
light to dark depends on the importance required by the parts of
the picture. The lack of a well-defined scheme of light and dark
is ruinous to any pictorial composition.

INDEX

96